*A
Little
Witch
in
Waiting*

FIRST EDITION

ISBNs
978-1-7391945-0-5 (paperback)
978-1-7391945-1-2 (hardback)
978-1-7391945-2-9 (eBook)

Claire Palmer

A Little Witch in Waiting

Illustrated by
Larch Gallagher

For Jess, Charles & George
you each have your own unique magic

- CP

For Lyra, and bump, and Jack
without you I would be lost

- LG

Contents

Introduction

This book of magical stories about a little Witch is intended for any age.

The stories follow on, one after each other.

You can read this book as a complete story, in the usual way, one chapter after the other. Alternatively, you can dip into it and read a chapter at random and see what emerges for you.

At the back of the book, there are reflective questions. Choose to answer after each chapter you read or at the end of the book. Alternatively, completely ignore that section. Choose what feels right for you.

Allow yourself to be immersed.

CHAPTER ONE

A Witch in Waiting

She sits so still by the fire. You would almost think she is a statue, a little doll in a beautiful English cottage.

But no – she moves, her legs swinging back and forth rhythmically. The rest of her is completely still. A tall, pointy witch's hat atop her red curls. Arms and legs encased in stripy woolly material beneath a short black pinafore dress.

'*Be in the stillness,*' they said, she muttered inside her head. This is so hard to do.

'*Allow it to emerge,*' they said.

For goodness sake, how can that happen?

Her small face contorted in concentration. This seemed so difficult.

The others knew how to do it. Well, not all. There were

lots of other little girls who didn't even know about this stuff. They didn't even know it existed.

Life must be simpler for them, she thought.

The small black dog at her feet stirred.

"What's to be done, Luna?" she asked her. Luna just looked at her with her beautiful doleful eyes.

I am thinking, I am concentrating, I am ignoring all those who doubt but nothing is happening. Absolutely nothing!

She felt the tears coming up, waiting to emerge and roll down her freckly face. She squeezed her eyelids together tightly, rocking her legs back and forth even faster now. She was NOT going to cry.

She was not!

She heard the wind gusting again outside. Suddenly the door swung open as if thrust by an enormous force. With equal speed it slammed shut again.

Perched on the dresser in a flurry of smoke or mist, she couldn't tell which, was a small bird, legs askance, chest puffed out, feathers somewhat ruffled. A mix of blues, purples and reds with eyes that bulged out.

She stared at the bird. Piercingly blue eyes stared back at her through the mist. A very deep voice for such a small bird came from its bright yellow beak.

"You really need to chill." The words bounced around the small room. "It comes from within."

She stared. Her legs were no longer swinging. Luna appeared transfixed.

"Suspend everything you think you know as truth. It WILL emerge," came the booming voice. More mist, and the ruffled feathers twitched.

"The stillness is within you. You will start to feel it inside. I know it is discomforting knowing that somehow you are different. Unsure how or what that means. It will be OK. Look, it's starting to feel different."

Her focused concentration had disappeared with the appearance of the bright bird, now she observed something bubbling within her. Was that just queasiness?

"Just be with it. Less concentration in the mind, more noticing within." With those words, the colourful, smoke-laden bird whizzed back out right through the keyhole. All that remained in the room were a few wisps of smoke.

She sat still in the chair, Luna by her feet. Her legs weren't swinging anymore. She adjusted her tall pointy hat and smiled.

CHAPTER TWO

A Dancing Witch

The music comes through.

She feels her feet tip tapping on her high stool. She can feel the beat through her body. Her pointy hat starts to jiggle back and forth as her body sways.

The little witch jumps down from the stool. She seems to have been perched there for a long, long time. She taps her tiny feet on the pine floor, throws her arms up in the air and dances. It feels so joyful. She didn't realise that sound and movement could produce such joy.

She bounces, dances around the pine table, just going with the sheer joy of it all. Around and around. No

one is watching. What was that expression? Dance like no one is watching. Was there more to it? The thoughts pop up as she twirls and bounces around the small room. She hears trumpets, bass, and a soulful sound. She bounces, jigs, twirling herself around, arms up high.

She catches a movement at her latticed window. Three small faces? They disappear as she stops moving, then slowly, as she watches, one by one they pop up again. Three round, wide-eyed faces stare at her. As if all statues, completely frozen. She looks at them. They look at her.

She doesn't dare move. Will they run away? Will she scare them? Is she frightened of them?

Slowly, slowly she smiles at them. They continue to stare and tentatively smile back.

Slowly, slowly as if she might frighten them, or herself, she walks to the door. Unlatching the heavy wooden door, she peers around the outside wall. The three faces are still there, now facing her. Slightly smaller than her and so different. No pointy hat, no striped socks. All dressed in different tones of green, matching scarves and hats and black boots. Their faces a little lined, hair sticking out beneath the green hats.
She smiles, retracing her steps, leaving the door open as she goes back in the cottage.

Once inside, she continues to dance. A little self-consciously, she feels the rhythm work through her. Her arms, legs, body moving in time to the music as she dances, filled with joy again.

She sees the three in green tentatively standing in the door frame.

She holds out her hand and slowly one of them steps forward and takes it. Rather like a wave motion she feels the connection.

The movement goes through her arm and down through the green arm. The small figure is moving in rhythm to the sound too. He stretches out a hand to the other two still watching at the door.

As one steps forward to hold his hand, the same thing happens. A wave-like motion passes between the three of them who are connected. They are all moving together as the last green figure jumps forward and joins on.

They are all connected and dancing around the table. Boots pounding as they land on the floor. It is tricky when they are all connected, almost as one person. Yet somehow it works. They get warmer and warmer as they move. No one wanting to let go.

When the music eventually stops, they all drop their hands and look at each other. What next?

The figures in green take a bow, in unison as if on a stage, then neatly and in step with each other walk out of the door. The last one with a hop and a skip and a wave of his hand in farewell, closing the door behind him as he leaves.

A Little Witch on her Path

She felt ready to explore. Where to? How to go about it?

She jumped from her high stool, running to look out of the small cottage window, her small pointy hat jiggling atop her red curls.

The English country landscape outside veered away down the hill. A small winding, pebbled path started at her front door then went off in many different directions.

Above the green fields ahead, the sky was blue but the clouds – wow – they looked so different! The clouds were a collage of colours, faces, words. Rather like newspapers all screwed up. Within the clouds she noticed large faces, all different yet all seemingly blowing out more clouds, like smoke.

She had no idea how that happened.

"Hmm," she muttered. Her little dog Luna looked up

expectantly. "Well, let's go and see, shall we?"

With a deep breath, she opened the heavy wooden door. The air outside was fresh, chilly like early morning spring. She took a firm step on the path. The 'funny' clouds were around, spinning back and forth, some close by, almost overhead. They were so close she could read the words on some, others the pictures. They were distracting and ominous. She had a real sense of dread as she just stood and stared at them all.
She stood transfixed by the movement, the words, the pictures, the activity. Time stood still until, looking so far skywards, her pointy witchy hat fell right off! Luna barked and jumped. The spell was broken.

She grabbed her hat, pulling it firmly down on her head, adjusted her black tunic, stood taller, shoulders back, and started walking. Her legs in stripy, woolly material stepping out confidently. She observed the clouds that continued to move back and forth.

Blooming attention-grabbing clouds, she thought to herself. *It's clear they're here as a distraction. Attention-grabbing headlines. Are they real? Invented? Does it matter? I can't grab hold of them or push them away.*

As she walked, they came in front of her, threatening to envelope her in mist. She tried ignoring them, but it did not help. Blow? Push? Ah ha! She realised she could push them away. She could gently grab hold and push them aside, rather like party balloons. She still noticed them, but she could follow the path without too much distraction now. Just the pushing away. The feeling of dread eased slightly.

She remembered the words from that bird with the bulgy eyes. *What was he called?* she wondered in passing.

"Just be with it. Less concentration in the mind, more noticing within."

As she spoke these words to herself, she noticed the clouds stopped a little of their careening back and forth. They almost seemed to retreat a little.

With her little black dog by her side, she stepped forward again on the path. Stripy legs moving with more ease.

CHAPTER THREE (PART TWO)

The Interlude

The little witch hadn't known where to go next. She had stepped out on her path for a while and then retraced her steps. Something hadn't felt quite right that time. It had felt important to notice.

Was it the right time now? Did she have the knowledge, the awareness? What was it she needed? She did not have a clue. Maybe nothing was needed. Maybe something critical. Who knows? Probably no one.
She had danced with some delightful green folk. Great fun, but still no clearer.

She was back on her high stool, looking out of the window.

The weather had changed.

The clouds had gone.

The little witch ventured to the door. She poked her

head out, looking one way and the other. She saw the path down the hill. The other way she saw a path too.

There were fir trees standing tall. There were other trees between and below them. The whole view was of beautiful autumnal shades with the darker fir trees highlighting different shades of bronze, gold, and red. There was a gentle breeze. The leaves from the autumnal trees were coming down like sparkles. Fluttering golden, twisting shimmering speckles.

She called her little black dog. Luna was already ahead of her, nose to the ground.

She closed her front door firmly behind her.

She stepped on the path again but going in a different direction.

There were bright blue skies way up high, way above the tops of the fir trees.

There was a chill in the air.

The sparkly golden leaves were still falling. The birds were singing.

As she walked, she spotted a small deer that trotted off between the trees. She had not heard it, nor did it seem bothered by her. A little

brown head and a disappearing white fluffy bottom.

The sea.

She could hear it. Waves crashing against rocks. It must be way, way down below.

She journeyed on, the crash of the waves accompanying her.

The trees parted a little. Those to her right were very twisted. They all leaned one way, towards the slope as if greeting her. They looked like people with many long extending arms.

Beyond the trees she could see the deep blue of the sea. Pure white waves that continued to crash against rock somewhere below her.

She could see birds above her. A dozen or so. They swirled together. Floating on the wind. Somehow, they knew when to turn and which way. Perfectly in unison. Ahead she could see buildings, little pink and white cottages by the sea. Sparkling water.

There was less of a noise now. More a gentle lapping.

The trees were still alongside her.

The soft path below turned harder. It was now rock. Solid yet slippery.

Suddenly the trees ended. She was still on the rocky path which now continued downward, onto a beach of the tiniest pebbles and shells. The path continued through the tall rocks ahead on the beach.

She noticed the birds above, still floating on the wind. Between the rocks ahead, she could just see a small turquoise boat bobbing on the sea.

CHAPTER FOUR

The Storm

The little witch had expected a short boat trip along the coastline.

She now found herself in a small boat out in very rough water. She could see others at sea but far away in various vessels, boats, yachts, dinghies. There was a storm all around that was twisting, turning in velocity and direction.

It changed frequently. She would be going in one direction for a few minutes and then around she spun in the opposite direction with no clear sight of land. There were moments of calmness when she thought she could see a distant view of land but then – no – it changed again.

Each time the wind picked up she pulled her pointy hat on even tighter. It was in real danger of flying off into the choppy waters. Her little black dog lay as close to the hull of the boat as she could, her ears flat to her head, sorrowful eyes looking up at her.

Witches were not used to being in a boat, she reflected. She did not have a clue what to do other than hang onto the tiller. Was it called that? she wondered. She wasn't sure she could do much anyway. Just hang on!

She caught a glimpse of land again, a faint green and blue colour then with a quick spin around, it was gone.

The whirling and the bobbing up and down seemed to go on forever. The little witch gripping on with tight hands, the little black dog lying as flat as possible next to her feet. Rather surprisingly, no water came into the

boat, just the buffeting and the spinning continued.

She could feel the queasiness well up. She breathed deep. One breath for the count of four, hold for two, a breath out for the count of seven. She repeated it. The spinning continued.

She focused on her breathing as best she could, holding onto the boat and trying to keep the rising panic at bay.

Then, as quickly as she had found herself on the choppy water with a storm around, everything changed.

She was alongside a steep muddy bank with green grass on top. Her legs felt so unsteady as she stepped off onto solid land. Her little back dog jumped out shaking herself vigorously before running around in circles sniffing the grass.

She straightened her black tunic, smoothed her stripy socks and checked to see if her hat was still there. Everything seemed to be in order. Yet she felt mighty strange.

Everything looked familiar and yet brighter. More vibrant. The birds were louder, chirpier. There was a small robin flying from branch to branch on a nearby tree. His birdsong was so loud and continuous as if she was meant to understand.

She stood and stared, noticing her wobbly legs.

Well, she wondered. *Could she make sense of it all? Was she meant to?*

She had to sit down.

She knelt, looked skyward and listened to the robin and the birds all around in the trees.

CHAPTER FIVE

The Walk up the Hill

She had been sitting on the soft green grass for a while now. The little witch felt better, her stomach was no longer queasy, her heart was beating at a normal pace. She noticed her legs were aching from being in the same position.

She jumped up, shook them out, observing her slightly green knees on her usual stripy legs. Her little black dog Luna was racing around, relishing the variety of new scents on the ground, blissfully happy. The birds were singing loudly, the trees looked as still as ever.

It really was not clear to her where she was going next. She could see no clear path through the trees. Everywhere looked like forest. The forest floor a dark brown beneath the trees.

I guess I'd better do something, she thought. *I can't stay here forever.*

She pulled her hat down atop her red curls and stepped forward, tentatively walking towards the trees, noticing as she went the groups of small birds that chirped and flew close to her. They swirled around joyfully. There was a small yet very fluffy robin who sat on one of the branches of the trees. It was so still and quiet she had missed it. She knew a robin was a good sign and she felt her heart do a tiny jump for joy.

As she got closer, the forest looked less intimidating. There was a huge, gnarled trunk of an old oak she could now see. The trunk looked like faces with long arms stretched wide out inviting or perhaps beckoning her in.

She could see ferns uncurling as she glanced into the

woods. She could make out a dark path through the ferns and trees. Luna was standing at the entrance to the path, the robin was sitting high up on a branch further along.

Am I following signs? she wondered. *How can I know?*

She felt compelled to go this way despite having no idea of her destination or intent. She could hear the voices in her head:

Surely you know where you are going?

You need to have a plan.

You look like you've got no direction.

This is such an odd way to go about anything.

Ridiculous!

Most people are not even here. They are content where they are.

She could hear them as she stood still. She was accustomed to them being with her. Determinedly she chose to ignore them. She concentrated on her feet and the path through the ferns.

She stepped forward and Luna ran happily ahead. The little robin flew off as she got closer. The way ahead was a clear path through ferns, past the large oak and straighter, more youthful trees. It meandered as it went.

The ancient woodland seemed to surround her, and she lost sight of the grassy bank behind. She noticed it was immensely peaceful. The smell of slightly damp woodland created a sense of well-being as the little witch walked along.

This feels so right, she thought to herself.

Onward and, she noticed, slightly upward she went.

CHAPTER SIX

Up, Up & Away

The path, soft underfoot with pine needles everywhere, continued upward.

The little witch was surrounded by very tall pine trees. The trunks were a rich brown colour beautifully textured with deep grooves in them. She could see the light of the sky way up high but within this part of the wood it was dark and silent. The light green ferns had gone. The flowers had disappeared. It was damp and silent everywhere.

I could go back.

She dismissed that thought quickly. It had taken her a long time to get here. She hoped she would reach somewhere soon. Surely. She did not know where that somewhere was or how she would know when she reached it. Instinctively she felt she would know.

She was tired and hungry. Luna, her black dog, no

longer racing around, trotted ahead of her.

It was silent everywhere. Spookily so. Even her feet were quiet on the ground as she walked.

She felt on edge, alert to every tiny noise.

On and on the path went.

Up and up.

On and on.

Up and up.

On and on.

She heard birds squawking up high.

Was she going to reach somewhere at last?

As if by magic, the trees stopped. She had come to a field, marked by hedges all around. In the near distance, she could see a small white cottage. Beyond that, all she could see were rolling hills. Miles and miles of rolling hills, fields, and hedges. It reminded her of a patchwork quilt in varying shades of greens and browns.

She so hoped there would be a friendly soul in that cottage. She was now really tired, hungry, and thirsty.

The walk across to the cottage was slightly downhill and the grass was short. There was a wide, stone-covered track coming into the walled garden, then a pebbled path leading towards the front door. It was just the type of door she had expected – an oak door with a large, heavy, brass knocker. Overhead a wooden porch, all surrounded by pink and very fragrant climbing roses. Next to it and underneath a window was a small bench. She knocked on the door and sat down. Bliss!

A flurry of swifts or swallows flew around the small bushes in front of her. A dance they all seemed to know. As she sat a fluffy, yet rather bedraggled robin landed on the arm of the seat. The little witch observed it before that too darted off.

She sat patiently then knocked louder. As she sat down again, she smelt the beautiful fragrance of sweet peas from a large earthenware planter nearby.

Perhaps no one is home. What shall I do then?

She could feel the tears and disappointment that were close to spilling out.

Turning to look, she realised the door was ajar, it was opening slowly and silently. Yet there was no one to be seen. A tiny weeny mouse shot out from the blackness within and scurried to the bushes.

CHAPTER SEVEN

Inside the Cottage

The little witch felt glued to the bench outside the cottage. She was weary. She was hungry. The door into the cottage was open yet she hesitated to go through. Somehow, she did seem to be stuck.

Gingerly she stood up and ventured towards the door. She knocked on the big door, noticing that the knocker was a heavy and beautiful brass bee.

"Anyone there?"

No answer.

Oh well. I have nothing to lose. And I am so hungry.

She ventured inside.

It was so much darker inside. There was light coming from a window on the stairs ahead and her eyes slowly adjusted to the lack of sunshine. There was a beautifully

decorated grandfather clock on the wall ahead, pictures on the whitewashed wall, an umbrella stand, coats on hooks and wellington boots, neatly arranged on the floor nearby.

She felt the welcome despite the silence. She could see two doors off the hall and the stairs ahead. Through one of the doors, she saw a large wooden table and a white sink.

"Hello?" Her voice sounded stronger.

Still no answer.

Her black dog Luna had been right by her side. She was now in the kitchen, obviously feeling more at home. It sounded like she was munching on dog biscuits!

Pushing the door open there was indeed a small brown bowl on the floor in the corner. There was even a bowl of water too. The contents of the brown bowl were being consumed loudly and with great speed.

The wooden table was laid for one, beautiful china, cutlery, and a crystal water glass with matching jug. A pie, steaming vegetables, a small loaf of bread, and golden cubes of butter.

There was a note on the plate: *Please enjoy the food and rest. This is for you to replenish yourself. There will be something for you afterwards but for now - eat well and enjoy.*

There was a small drawn image of a little mouse at the bottom.

How wonderful!

She sat down and helped herself, relishing the smells and tastes as she ate. When she felt ever so slightly full, she wandered through to the other room downstairs. It seemed rude to go upstairs.

There was a wonderful comfy settee in the lounge. Bliss! She could sit and put her feet up. As she did so, the little witch noticed another note on the small table where she had placed her glass of water:

At the end of the note was another small mouse. A mouse with a very long tail, that wrapped its way around the page and seemed to point to an almost empty shelf on the bookcase nearby. She could see a beautiful red book.

It was full of blank pages.

Questions and thoughts formed in her head like bubbles rising to the surface.

Why am I being asked that question? Am I meant to write? What's the point? Is that an important question? It feels like it is, and I haven't got a clue where to even start.

CHAPTER EIGHT

Reflections

The little witch woke up with a start.

She realised she had fallen asleep on the beautiful blue velvet settee. A red book was on her lap.

It felt as if she had been asleep for a long, long time. She knew that she had been busy doing something.

What was it? Was it important? She had no idea.

As she rubbed her eyes, she spotted a white piece of paper on the floor.

What is important to know right now?

That was the question then. That explained why she had fallen asleep. She felt a heaviness return to her shoulders.

She noticed there was a fire crackling in the grate, small candles lit up the shelves and the corners of the room. It was so cosy. A soft, grey blanket had been placed over her as she slept.

Who had come in?

She sat up, stretched, then immediately pulled the warm blanket tight around her and settled back again. She noticed her small black dog was curled up in front of the fire.

She wondered what to do. She was confused. The piece of paper was in her hand now. She had screwed it up. She smoothed it out on her knee. It felt such a large, difficult question. She didn't know what she was supposed to know.

How would she know what she was supposed to know? Was it important? Was it a fact, a feeling or something completely different? On an impulse she screwed the paper into a ball and threw it towards the fire. It landed on top of her black dog Luna who looked up, startled.

As if by magic, the red book and pen appeared to be closer to her, almost demanding she wrote. As she sat wrapped up in her blanket, the pen had a life of its own. Her eyes widened as she saw the words form on the page.

The knowing is not facts or feelings, although they are a part. It is important to know, at a deep level, that you are on a path. Trust yourself even more. All is as it is meant to be.

The writing was slanting, long letters and italic. Beautiful, as if from an ancient book.

The little witch felt as if a great weight had been lifted from her shoulders. She felt lighter and warmer as she snuggled down with the blanket around her.

She looked around the room, noticing again the little candles. The whole room felt so warm and cosy, like a snug nest.

The little witch saw that it was snowing outside. Through the large window, she could see big fluffy snowflakes falling. It looked magical out there, a winter wonderland.

She put another log on the fire, watching the flames grow and dance as if they were little figures. Feeling warmer, she wandered around the room, noticing the books on the shelves, picking up one or two that looked interesting, then returning them to their original place. They were beautiful too. Rich, dark colours as if they were chosen for their beauty alone.

She noticed the falling snow had stopped. Outside, just visible against the far trees she could see movement. It looked like the snow was lifting and moving on its own. She put her face close to the window, feeling the chill as she did so. There WAS movement, she could not see what it was but the snow itself was moving in some way.

CHAPTER NINE

The Angel

The little witch was fascinated by the view through the window. The window itself was small panes of glass. Looking through one of the small panes, she could see

the light outside had the orange glow that a sky full of snow creates.

She could feel the warmth of the room behind her, the fire crackling, the candles flickering. She felt again the chill as she pushed her nose closer to the glass so she could see even better.

Thick snow was everywhere, covering the ground in large mounds. The trees were laden. Everything was still. Yet close to the trees there was movement. It was so difficult to make out a shape or colour. She could sense a presence of something. She felt the anxiety in her stomach.

As if she sensed it too, her little black dog jumped up onto the large window ledge next to her. Like a cat she wanted a stroke and she too needed to look out of the window.

The little witch reached down to pull up her long stripy socks, tightening the grey blanket around her even more. As she turned back to the snowy scene outside her window, she saw a pattern in the smooth snow.

She felt her heart leap. There was a clear shape of an angel in the crystal and previously perfect snow. As if someone had lain down in the fresh snow and moved their arms up and down.

She looked back and forth to see if she could see anything. Nothing. No footprints on the snow at all. Just the shape.

Her heart was beating fast and hard. She could feel it inside her chest. She took slow, steady breaths, feeling it slow down. She continued to stroke her dog who was surprisingly quiet and still. She was at a loss what to do next. It felt very scary, and cold, to venture outside. She was just drawn to look at the image on the ground.

As she stood, somewhat transfixed, the shape moved.

How is that even possible?

It was as if it was made from fine, uncooked pastry. It looked like it lifted off the snow and was suspended and floating above the snow. The little witch was transfixed. Her little dog Luna started barking and barking at the apparition through the window. She too wasn't sure what to make of what she was seeing either, so she just barked and barked.

The angel floated and twisted away towards the far trees. Almost a hover. Almost transparent, definitely white with large wings.

Oddly enough the little witch didn't feel frightened now. She raced outside grabbing a coat, a fluffy wool hat and scrambling for boots from the collection in the hall. They were enormous but warm. They would do. Her pointy witchy hat was tucked away in her pinafore.

As she stepped outside, the icy cold took her breath away and yet she wasn't frightened. Despite the cold, she felt as if there was a warm and friendly presence waiting for her.

CHAPTER TEN

Through the Woods

She ran through the thick, untouched snow. It was so much harder than she imagined. She could see the angel-like shape ahead of her. It seemed to be dancing and twisting through the trees.

Her little black dog Luna bounced through the snow close to her. The snow was so deep, she seemed to disappear as she landed only to reappear as she jumped again.

She was close to the tall fir trees she had seen from

the window. The snow was less dense here. Her running became much easier. So much easier now she felt solid earth beneath her feet and her legs could move freely.

She had come to a halt as she had lost sight of the floating, twisting angel ahead of her. There was nothing but dense fir trees.

Luna was racing around the tree trunks, sniffing. Delighted to have freedom too. She had small ice balls attached to her feet and ears, yet she seemed unfazed by them, just occasionally shaking her head as if to dislodge them from her floppy, black ears.

The little witch pulled up her stripy socks, pulled down the woolly hat that she had grabbed from the cottage, and took a deep breath. She focused on the earth beneath her feet and that felt important. To feel her feet firmly planted on the ground.

She spun around, twisting and turning, looking for the opaque angel. She couldn't see her at all. She wandered slowly through the trees. The orange glow from the sky lit up the darkness.

Everywhere was so still, so silent. The only sound she could hear was her dog as she raced from place to place. The crispy brittle leaves rustling as she ran.

The little witch considered retreating to the cottage as the excitement seemed to be over. She took a quick look around through the trees and turned back the way she had come. She could only see trees every way she looked.

There was a distinct path here, she thought. *Or at least there were my footprints in the snow.*

Nothing.

It was as if everything had closed in and filled up from where she had been. Even Luna's footprints were no longer visible. The fir trees were dense in every direction. She felt her heart drop.

This feels very scary, I feel so alone within these strange fir trees.

She could still feel the earth beneath her. It was comforting to know, and it felt very real and solid. She took another long breath and focused on the ground beneath her. As she did, she felt a presence behind her back. She had a glimpse of the angel as she spun around and as she got that glimpse, it seemed to disappear.

It was like a shadow right behind her, yet she could only get the tiniest of sightings. As she continued to spin around each way, trying to get more of a sighting, her dog sat watching her. Luna seemed not the slightest part bothered by what might be there.

The little witch gave up her spinning and decided the

angel WAS behind her, she just couldn't see her. With
that knowledge she felt safer as she took a tentative step
forward.

CHAPTER ELEVEN

Where Next?

She felt that she had been in the dense fir trees for a long, long time. There had been no path and yet deep down the little witch felt she had been going the 'right' way.

The weather had gotten warmer. She had discarded her woolly hat a long time ago. Her black pointed hat was back on top of her red curls.

Way up above, beyond the tall treetops, she could see blue skies. Soft, fluffy clouds passing through.

The trees thinned out a little. Between the trees there were ferns. Tall, fresh green ferns that came up to her shoulders. Ferns that seemed to be uncurling and growing taller as she walked. There was now a thin path of brown earth that weaved its way between the ferns.

Every so often the path would widen to encompass a tree along its way. These trees were ancient. Wide, majestic tree trunks that reached way up high. Branches spreading wide. Oaks and yews, occasionally horse chestnuts. The trunks like friendly faces smiling at her.

As she came to one glade, she was surprised to see a man walking towards her. A tall, slightly stooped, grey-haired man with a small rucksack. Luna raced excitedly towards him. Another human!

As the little witch had only been used to speaking to her little dog, she had almost forgotten the sound of her own voice.

"Hello," she said croakily.

"Afternoon," he said. "Can you tell me where this path goes to? I'm hoping to catch the four o'clock bus."

The little witch's face must have registered her surprise as the man looked at her with puzzlement and a slight frown.

"I am sorry, I have no idea. Where are you wanting to go?"

"Oh, it's the circular bus. I like to turn up and catch it when I can." With a parting smile the tall man strode off.

Ahead of her, next to the tall oak was a small wicker basket with a large label – 'For the little witch'. She spun around wondering who else was close by. No sound and no one. The woods were as quiet as ever. Luna had her nose in the basket already.

The little witch sat down, leant against the tree, and tucked in. Egg sandwiches, baby tomatoes, an apple, small scones with jam inside, and a little bottle of lemonade. Luna had her own mix of cheese and doggie biscuits. Wonderful!

After a little snooze, they were both ready to go. To where, the little witch had no idea.

She adjusted her tall, pointed hat, smoothed her black tunic down, pulled up her stripy socks and set off again. The path continued through the tall ferns.

The ferns were as tall as ever, yet she could clearly see that the path meandered down a gentle slope. She passed an ancient yew tree on her left. A robin sang on one of the branches. Unfazed by the little witch's presence, it flew off landing on a tree further ahead on the path.

Down and down the little witch walked, her little dog racing ahead.

CHAPTER TWELVE

The Pool

The little witch had found so much to enjoy as she journeyed downhill. She had met people sitting having food on a blanket. Then a large group dancing. Another group with a tiny baby, celebrating a new life. There seemed to be so much joy. Yet there had been groups with great sadness. She felt it in her soul. It was as if she had seen all facets of life as she traversed the hillside.

The earlier forest had given way to a grassy incline with occasional flatter areas where she found the groups of people amidst the shelter of trees. She had stopped to speak to them all. Her little dog had raced to meet them too, enjoying the attention.

They were welcomed by each group. The children had been fascinated by her pointy hat and stripy socks. She had laughed, eaten some food and listened to their stories. They were all there to mark a special event in their lives. The little witch noticed how much she had missed conversation and connection. There was fun to be had despite the journey and the learnings.

As she continued downhill, she could hear the faint sound of gurgling water. It gradually increased in volume. The sporadic trees started to merge and come together to form a small woodland area going down the hillside. The wood was nowhere near as dense as she had travelled through before.

There were numerous paths through the trees and the trees themselves were just starting to lose the denseness of summer. Some of the leaves were slightly dry and yellow, the ferns were brown-tinged. A robin flew ahead of her again, darting from branch to branch. She was very happy to recognise that red breast. He seemed to be tracking her, or maybe he was leading her.

It had sounded as if it was a short journey down to the gurgling water that she had heard from further up. Like journeys before, it had taken much longer. The sound came from a waterfall. The water sprang out from further up the hillside, landing in a clear pool before bouncing and gurgling over large, round, smooth-shaped stones as it continued downwards through the trees.

The little witch sat on a large round stone close to the pool. The water was almost motionless, the trees and blue sky with clouds clearly reflected in the water. The sounds from the people scattered above on the hillside had faded. It was just her and Luna who was happily playing with a small stick under the trees.

As she sat looking into the pool the little witch could see her pointy hat and red curls reflected. Behind her she caught a glimpse of something white.

Her angel!

It was so joyful to know she was still there. She hadn't been left behind in the snow. She felt her heart sing even more and she smiled at the reflection in the still water. Out of the corner of her eye she saw two robins jumping about on the ground nearby.

As she sat on the hard stone and watched them, she had a strong sense she was on her way home.

CHAPTER THIRTEEN

Sadness

The little witch had felt she was on her way home and suddenly she had been overcome with sadness. It was like a well that she felt coming up from inside, from the very centre of her.

She had been sitting by the pool watching the robins and comforted by the awareness that her angel was close behind. She had felt such a sense of ease and tranquillity and then – *woosh*. The sadness had come.

She wanted to squash it down. Suppress it. Stop it from rising up and consuming her. It took energy and she could feel her body tense up in preparation, her mind analysing it, stopping it from becoming more solid so she could get on.

As she sat, she noticed all this and unlike other times, she waited, watched, and thought.

What would happen if she let it rise? Would she be ok?

She didn't know, but with her whole being she felt that it would be alright. She felt so connected to the earth. She felt supported. She relaxed as much as she could and let the sadness rise up. It rose up through her appearing as white cloud all around her. It was as if she was being surrounded by the smoke from a fire, or low-level cloud. It had no smell - just wispy soft cloud.

She stood up and retreated back from the pool. She felt the trunk of a tree behind her as she allowed the tears to flow.

Time passed. As the tears flowed, the mist stayed with her though oddly she found she could see more. Magically, the roots of the trees around her now seemed to be more obvious. It was as if she could feel them through the soil. There were so many roots. They looked to be communicating and the messages were now concentrated in the roots of the tree she was leaning against. She could feel warmth transmitting from her feet upwards.

The tears continued.

It felt so wonderful. The little witch stopped working it out and was just present to the tears, the tree roots and the warmth in her feet. She felt much more connected to her body, her felt sense. Her active mind was wanting to get engaged, she could hear her internal voice whispering, then getting louder. As if fighting to get heard. The little witch did her very best to ignore it. She concentrated on her physical body. Her feet, her arms, her legs, all of her.

As she did this, the tree roots somehow came together. Like a baby's cradle, a wicker basket formed for her. With the tree still behind her, she felt as if she was slipping yet still held in place. It felt incredibly soothing and supportive.

She was just still, held in this place. Her pointy hat somehow stayed on her head, and she could see her thin legs in stripy socks in front of her, her little black boots at the end. She rested.

Somehow, she found she was upright again. Her black boots were on the firm soil. The tree roots were back underground. The tears had passed. She felt ready to go. She was definitely on her way home.

CHAPTER FOURTEEN

Stepping Stones

As she left the pool behind and continued downhill, the little witch felt excited. She could see water again, a river. It meandered through the field and trees below. It was so much closer.

Down, down, down she went. Her little dog raced ahead of her.

It seemed to get cooler as she went down. Her friend the robin appeared now and again. Her dog bounced ahead, tail wagging madly as she found exciting scents along the way.

Completely unexpectedly, the river was in front of her. A fast-flowing river with a stone path alongside the bank. Reeds grew along the riverbank, and occasional trees with their roots in the water.

It wasn't a huge river but unpassable without a bridge. The water flowed fast, it was clear with a slight brown tinge and she could see occasional groups of fish. There was nowhere to go but along the path.

The river continued around the next corner of the hillside. Ahead and on the far side she could see a road and a bus stop! As she got closer, she saw there was someone waiting there. It was the man she had met in the woods! He was waving his arms around madly. She got the impression that he was hurrying her to get over to join him.

That was impossible. There was no way to do that. The river looked to go on forever and there was no way to get across.

The man was still waving her forward.

She moved down the riverbank, so she was opposite him, on her side of the river. If anything, the river was wider at this point but no less deep. She could see the stones at the bottom, but she knew it was too deep to wade across. She also knew her little dog was not too keen on swimming.

The man was still gesticulating. As she looked, she saw in the distance a red bus. It was way off but coming slowly along the road.

She looked at the water again.

Still the man waved her forward.

She couldn't hear what he shouted.

How could she step on water? She certainly couldn't walk or swim across. The water was flowing too fast.

As she saw the bus getting ever closer, she looked at the water. As she did so, she saw one of the larger stones rise up to the surface. Then another one. And another. Stepping stones!

The man on the other side was waving and encouraging her even more. The bus was closer.

The stones were now clearly seen in the river. Large and close enough for her to walk across.

They were wet and looked slippery, but her boots

were good. With her heart in her mouth and her dog alongside, she set off. Stepping one foot at a time and stopping on each stone, she went from one to the next.

Halfway across the river, the little witch felt her legs wobble. The water was rushing past the stones and the water below looked very dark. She could no longer see the bottom. She couldn't go back. With a huge, deep breath she stepped forward again. One foot forward then together. One foot forward then together.

She was on the other side, on the road. Her heart was beating fast, her legs still a little wobbly but she had made it. Her little black dog shook herself, she was glad to be away from the flowing water.

She looked back at the river and the stepping stones were slowly disappearing back under the water.

The little witch straightened the hat on her head and turned to face the man and the advancing bus.

CHAPTER FIFTEEN

The Bus

The little witch was surprised to see the tall man again.

"Hello, thanks for letting me know about getting across the river. It was very kind of you."

The tall man nodded and repeated the statement he had made the last time they met. "There is only a bus once a fortnight, at four o'clock. Glad you made it."

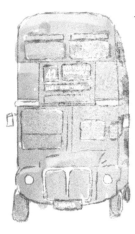

As he spoke, the bus arrived, a bright red bus with number 42 displayed at the front. It came to a slow stop next to them both. The driver, a pink-cheeked, white-haired lady, greeted the man and smiled at her as she climbed on board. As her dog passed her, she stretched out a beautifully manicured hand and stroked her.

There were no other people on the

bus. The man had retreated to the back so she took a seat near the front with Luna jumping onto the seat next to her.

"Home?" the driver asked the little witch as she looked at her through the bus mirror.

"Yes please," she replied quickly.

Both settled in their seats and off they went.

The bus meandered along the road close to the river. They were in a valley with steep hills either side. The river twinkled with sunlight. Soon the road left the river and wound its way up hill through a cattle grid, past stone brick walls and up onto moorland.

The little witch could see for miles. No trees, just moorland with heather and gorse bushes. She saw sheep scattered across the moor between the purple heather. Little white dots as far as she could see.

The moors went on forever. As well as the sheep she could see horses of many varying colours.

Occasionally they would pass a small hamlet.

At one of the small hamlets, the tall man got off with a smile and a tip of his hat.

She must have dozed off, her little dog's head on her lap. When she looked out of the window the landscape had changed. It was now a low sunset and the moorland had changed to green hills. It looked familiar.

The little witch caught the driver's eyes in the mirror.

"All well sweetie?" the white-haired lady asked. "Did you have a good trip? Did you go where you wanted to go? Find what you were looking for?"

"I had a lovely time, thank you," said the little witch. "I went to some amazing places, but I am not sure what I was looking for, so I don't know if I found it."

The little witch stroked the head of her little black dog, looked at the passing scenery and thought to herself. That statement was true, and she certainly couldn't articulate what was different, yet she felt something had changed.

It was as if she was stepping back into the world, but she was seeing things differently. Was that true? Perhaps she was just more aware of what was not so clearly seen or heard.

She sat pondering this until she heard the driver shout, "Your stop, sweetie!"

The bus came to a sudden stop.

CHAPTER SIXTEEN

Homecoming

She raced to get off the bus, her little black dog at her heels.

"Thanks so much," she called to the driver as she jumped off the bus. Giving her a wave as she did so.

I am almost home. She felt a warm glow of anticipation come up through her whole body.

Her little black dog Luna knew exactly where she was. She had raced up the winding, pebbled path, and was now stopped at the gate ahead.

The little witch felt her heart beating as she saw her cottage ahead. Lights were twinkling through the window and there was smoke coming out of the chimney.

As she unlatched the little gate, she realised there were people wandering through her garden. It was a wonderful garden party. There was bunting and beautiful

pink flowery triangles. Lights in the trees and shrubs.

Everyone had a glass of something pink. These were all people she recognised, her friends, her family. Some were still in this world, others had left. Some hugged her. Some just seemed to pass right through her. Others whispered, "Lovely to see you."

Luna was racing around all over the garden. She was running as fast as she could in circles, full of excitement.

The little witch felt tears in her eyes. Tears of joy. She was loved so much. It was wonderful to see all these familiar faces.

The little witch adjusted her pointy hat atop her red curls, took a glass when it was offered from a passing hand, and then spent time greeting each person.

As time went on, those who were not in this world seemed to hover and fade but still she felt their presence. The essence of them was with her.

As all of her other friends and family happily chatted in the garden, she walked to the front door and looked in. Everything was as she had left it. As if she had never been away. Perhaps she hadn't. Her high stool was there, where she loved to sit and swing her legs. Everything looked the same and yet, things were different.

She wandered around her cottage then sat on the high stool and swung her stripy legs.

Her little black dog, weary from the excitement, curled up at her feet.

As she sat, she was conscious of a robin singing on top of a branch by her open window. As she turned, she caught a glimpse of white behind her and out of the corner of her eye. The little witch knew things had changed for her.

For now, she settled back home.

Journaling Prompts

Chapter One: A Witch in Waiting

What message(s) do you hear?

Whose voices do you listen it? In what way are they helpful? Or unhelpful?

Chapter Two: A Dancing Witch

What brings you joy?

How can you have more of it in your life?

Who brings you joy?

Chapter Three: A Little Witch on Her Path

What are you drawn to do?

What is inviting you?

What is distracting you?

Chapter Three (Part Two): The Interlude

What do you notice as your days pass?

What might you have missed?

Chapter Four: The Storm

What 'storms' have you survived?

Which personal strengths helped you?

Chapter Five: The Walk up the Hill

What, if anything, are you putting off?

What would happen if you trusted you knew what to do?

What is one small step?

Chapter Six: Up, Up and Away

What would happen if you let go of control? Of being certain of what might happen.

Could you take a risk?

What needs to happen?

Chapter Seven: Inside the Cottage

What occurs to you after reading this story?

What is important to you now?

Chapter Eight: Reflections

What would change if you rested for a while?

What would change if you changed your pace?

Chapter Nine: The Angel

What does the angel represent to you?

What difference would it make if you had an angel with you?

Chapter Ten: Through the Woods

What does 'keeping your feet on the ground' mean to you?

If you knew (or pretended) you were always supported, what difference would it make?

Chapter Eleven: Where next?

What are you grateful for? List as many things as possible, however tiny you think they might be.

What else occurs to you after reading this story?

Chapter Twelve: The Pool

What 'signs' might you be missing?

What can you see, hear, sense or feel?

Chapter Thirteen: Sadness

What might you be sad about?

What difference does it make to focus on your body rather than your thoughts?

Chapter Fourteen: Stepping Stones

If you left what you were struggling to find an answer for, took some time away, what might emerge?

Can you trust that there will be a solution?

Who or what might help you?

Chapter Fifteen: The Bus

What can you see from afar?

What else occurs to you after reading this story?

Chapter Sixteen: Homecoming

What difference does loving others and being loved make to you?

How could you alter things, so you really notice, feel and share that love?

From all the stories, what is the most important
message you have taken for yourself?

Acknowledgements

My thanks to Martha Beck who started this off with her amazing Write into Light programme and for so much more. My wonderful WIL buddies, Karen MB, Dana, Karen F, Ceri, Stephanie, Mary, Shanti who were there right from the start. Ben Jones who had the skill, patience to get this out to the world. Thank you all so much for your support and wisdom along the way.

Pamela Richarde for your encouragement and belief, Louise for your kindness and support. Cathy and Laura B for your wise words and perspectives.

Thanks to all my coaching pals, clients, friends who have all made a positive impact along the way.

I am deeply grateful for finding Larch, a complete star, who created delightful illustrations that matched what was in my head. You are amazing; it was such a delight working with you. Many, many thanks.

Finally, Graham for always providing the love and support – no matter what I do!

About the Author

Claire Palmer has worked as a Coach for over twenty years, enabling transformational change for her clients who are worldwide. Previously she worked as a senior leader in a large financial organisation. Claire now combines her logic with her strong intuitive gifts. She started the first story for A little Witch in 2019 and the stories just emerged.

About the Illustrator

Larch Gallagher worked in primary schools almost her whole adult life before hopping into the world of publishing. She took a break to teach English, and eat sushi, in Japan, before returning home and beginning work as a freelance designer and illustrator. This is her first illustrated book to be published. She is very nervous and proud, and hopes you like it!

Ingram Content Group UK Ltd.
Milton Keynes UK
UKHW021052120323
418386UK00002B/41

9 781739 194512